TRUE CRIME

D0881412

COLD CASES

T. R. Thomas

SADDLEBACK
EDUCATIONAL PUBLISHING

TRUE CRIME

Celebrity Cases

Cold Cases

DNA Cases

Forensics

Serial Killers

SADDLEBACK
EDUCATIONAL PUBLISHING
www.sdlback.com

ISBN-13: 978-1-59905-437-7
ISBN-10: 1-59905-437-X
eBook: 978-1-60291-763-7

Printed in the U.S.A.

19 18 17 16 15   6 7 8 9 10

Photo Credits: Natalee Holloway, Nelson "Speedy" Andrad/epa/Corbis; Jam Master Jay,
Getty Images; Scott Peterson, Justin Sullivan/Pool/Reuters/Corbis; JonBenét Ramsey,
Koester Axel/Corbis Sygma

CONTENTS

Introduction 5

1 Jam-Master Jay 7

2 JonBenét Ramsey 18

3 Natalee Holloway 29

4 The Allen-Cutshall Murders 40

5 Solved at Last 51

Glossary 61

Index 63

INTRODUCTION

Detectives find cold cases frustrating. They hunt down clues. They interview suspects. Often all they find are dead ends. Eventually they have to give up. They file the case away.

Usually they keep the evidence. Sometimes police solve cases many years later. High-profile cold cases are splashed all over the news. This book is about cold cases.

Jam-Master Jay was a hip-hop pioneer. He was shot in 2002. Witnesses have not been very helpful. So far police have not solved the case.

JonBenét Ramsey was a six-year-old beauty queen. She was murdered on Christmas in 1996. Police accused her parents. Eventually a new kind of DNA test proved them wrong.

Natalee Holloway disappeared in 2005. She was on a high school graduation trip to Aruba.

Lindsay Cutshall, 22, and Jason Allen, 26, were sleeping on the beach in 2004. Someone shot them in their sleeping bags.

The last chapter covers two cold cases that police eventually solved. Chandra Levy was murdered in 2001. In 2009 police caught her murderer. Laci Peterson and her unborn son were killed on Christmas Eve in 2002. Police eventually had enough evidence to convict her husband, Scott. Chandra and Laci were both from Modesto, California.

CHAPTER 1
JAM-MASTER JAY

DATAFILE

T I M E L I N E

1983

Run-DMC is the first hip-hop album to go gold.

October 30, 2002

Jam-Master Jay is shot in Queens, New York.

April 2007

Police name Ronald "Tenad" Washington a suspect.

Where is Queens, New York?

KEY TERMS

accomplice—someone who helps commit a crime

blacklisted—added to a list of people kept from working in their field

inducted—made a member of a group through a formal ceremony

speculation—guesswork

uncooperative—not willing to work together toward a common goal

DID YOU KNOW?

Kenneth McGriff is a former Queens drug lord. He may have been involved in Jam-Master Jay's death. McGriff is now in prison for other crimes. He's doing life at ADX Florence. It's a super-maximum-security prison in Colorado. It is also home to the Shoe Bomber and other terrorists.

JAM-MASTER JAY

When Tupac Shakur and Biggie Smalls died, that was bad. But it was not completely unexpected. Their motto seemed to be "Live by the sword, die by the sword."

But Jam-Master Jay was different. He was no thug. He was a 37-year-old married man. He had three kids. He came from a middle-class background. His music reflected what was going on in the streets. But it wasn't what you'd call hardcore.

It was a huge shock when he was gunned down like a thug. Hip-hop fans mourned the loss.

Rapping in the Park

Jason Mizell was born in 1965 in Brooklyn, New York. His family moved to Hollis, in Queens, when he was 10.

As a young man, he started DJing at Two-Fifths Park in Hollis. Jason was called "Jazzy Jase" back then. Jase was the most popular DJ at the park. He was known for his flashy clothes. He also was one of the first to scratch vinyl on a turntable.

Jase had some trouble with the law as a teen. But he decided thug life wasn't for him. He liked music much better.

In 1980 he hooked up with Joseph "DJ Run" Simmons and Darryl "DMC" McDaniels. They first met at Two-Fifths Park. The three talented young men clicked

Run-DMC members (left to right) Joseph Simmons (Run), Darryl McDaniels (DMC), and Jason Mizell (Jam-Master Jay) pose for a May 1999 portrait in Los Angeles.

right away. They decided to form a group. That's how Run-DMC came to be.

Run-DMC: Hip-Hop Pioneers

Run-DMC was a smash right from the start. The group's sound was revolutionary. No one had heard it before. It had a hard beat. There was a rock flavor to it. Their first single, "It's Like That/Sucker MCs," started a rap revolution. They released it in 1983.

Before that, rap was heavily influenced by funk and disco. But Run-DMC's sound was different.

Their self-titled first album, *Run-DMC*, was the first rap album ever to go gold. That was in 1983. Their 1985 album *King of Rock* was the first ever platinum rap record.

Walk This Way!

Run-DMC got together with the rock band Aerosmith in 1986. They did a rap version of the Aerosmith's song "Walk This Way." The classic video featured both groups.

The song's success made Run-DMC's album *Raising Hell* their most successful ever. It was also one of the top-selling hip-hop albums of all time. It blurred the lines between rap and rock.

On April 4, 2009, Run-DMC was *inducted* into the Rock and Roll Hall of Fame.

Run-DMC Slows Down

Throughout the 1990s, Run-DMC performed less and less. Hip-hop was changing. The group was becoming outdated.

On his own, Jam-Master Jay had become a successful record producer. He founded his own label, JMJ Records. And he discovered several acts that did well. One was OnyX. They had a major success with their 1993 hit single "Slam."

In 2001 Run-DMC started off on a reunion tour with Aerosmith. But it just wasn't the same. The members had gone in different directions. They didn't even finish the tour.

Shot in Cold Blood

The three remained friends in spite of their differences. Run and DMC couldn't believe it when Jay was shot in 2002. No one could.

Jam-Master Jay was shot in cold blood on October 30, 2002. He was in his recording studio when it happened.

A female witness said she was near the studio entrance when the gunmen entered. The shooter had a tattoo on the back of his neck. He wore a black sweat suit. She said he walked over to Jay, and the two high-fived. They obviously knew each other. Then the tattooed man opened fire.

The first shot missed Jay. It hit Tony Rincon, who was nearby. The shot hit Rincon's ankle. He survived. The gunman then shot Jay in the head. This time he didn't miss.

The crime has never been solved.

In April 2007, however, police named a suspect. Police said Ronald "Tenad" Washington was an *accomplice*. That's someone who helps with a crime. The witness said Washington was the one who held a gun to her head. But he was not the one who killed Jam-Master Jay. The tattooed man did that, she said. But she never got a good look at his face.

All Because of a Song?

As of mid-2009, Jam-Master Jay's murder remains unsolved. Part of the problem is *uncooperative* witnesses. People may be afraid to talk.

There is some *speculation* that Kenneth "Supreme" McGriff may have been involved. He's a convicted drug lord with mob ties. McGriff is in prison for life for other crimes.

McGriff *blacklisted* hip-hop artist 50 Cent. It was because of his song "Ghetto Qu'ran." Qur'an is another spelling of *Koran.* That's the Islamic holy book.

The song talked about drug dealers from the 1980s. Some people think 50 Cent was a snitch. They think he shouldn't have named names in the song. In 2000, someone shot 50 Cent nine times. He survived. People wonder if McGriff's crew was behind that attempt on his life.

50 Cent has done very well as an artist. He's had several very successful albums.

Jam-Master Jay gave 50 Cent his start. He taught 50 Cent how to write music and make a record. So some say Jay was killed for helping 50 Cent. But that's purely speculation. No one really knows for sure, except the killer.

Hopefully one day the world will know, too.

CHAPTER 2
JONBENÉT RAMSEY

DATAFILE

T I M E L I N E

December 25, 1996

JonBenét Ramsey is murdered.

July 9, 2008

Police drop all charges against the Ramseys.

February 2, 2009

Boulder police reopen the case.

Where is Boulder, Colorado?

KEY TERMS

autopsy—a study done on a dead body to find the cause of death

garrote—a corded device with handles, used for strangling

jurisdiction—authority over an area's law enforcement

ligature—something used for tying someone up, such as rope or cord

touch DNA test—a new DNA test that can take a DNA sample from an item that was touched

DID YOU KNOW?

In August 2006, a man named John Mark Karr said he had killed JonBenét. But a DNA test proved he was not involved. He had made a false confession.

JONBENÉT RAMSEY

JonBenét Ramsey was a beautiful little girl. She had long blonde curls, huge blue eyes, and a sweet smile. She was a born entertainer. She loved to sing, dance, and swing her Hula-hoop.

She liked playing outside, too. She also took violin lessons. In many ways, JonBenét was like other six-year-olds. She had many friends at school.

Beauty contests made her seem special, though. She was like a little princess.

Her mother, Patsy, had also been a beauty contestant. In 1977 she was crowned Miss West Virginia. Patsy began entering beauty contests in high school. She got "pageant fever."

JonBenét seemed to have pageant fever, too. She was a seasoned pro by the time she was six. She had won many contests, including Little Miss Merry Christmas. The little girl adored pageants. She loved the excitement and the glamour.

JonBenét's Last Christmas

The Ramseys lived in a red brick mansion in Boulder, Colorado.

Christmas day 1996 was a happy one for the Ramseys. JonBenét and her brother, Burke, happily tore into their gifts. JonBenét got a bicycle from Santa. Their good friends, the Whites, had them over for Christmas dinner.

When the Ramseys got home, they were tired but happy. Patsy and her husband John put JonBenét to bed around 10:30 p.m.

It was the last time they saw her alive.

Kidnapped?

Patsy Ramsey came downstairs early the next morning. There was a three-page, handwritten letter at the bottom of the staircase. With dawning horror, Patsy realized it was a ransom note. Oddly, it asked for $118,000. That was the exact amount of John Ramsey's Christmas bonus.

There were other strange things about the note, too. Near the end, it said, "Don't try to grow a brain, John." That line is from the movie *Speed*. The note was signed "Victory! S.B.T.C." That may have been a satanic clue. Those initials stand for "Saved By The Cross."

The note said not to call police. But the Ramseys did anyway. They called the police and the FBI. They also called family and friends. They told people JonBenét had been kidnapped.

A Chilling Discovery

The police did a quick check. They found no signs of a break-in. At around 1 p.m. a detective decided to conduct a more thorough search. She asked John Ramsey and two friends to search the house. The detective told them to look for "anything unusual."

When they got to the wine cellar, they made a chilling discovery. It was JonBenét's lifeless body. Her body was under a white blanket. She had been murdered. There were *ligature* marks on her neck. She had been strangled with a *garrote.* Duct tape covered her mouth.

JonBenét Ramsey's murder shocks the nation.

But by then, the crime scene had been contaminated. Critics later said the police didn't do a good job that day. They had let people in and out of the house. They had not searched the neighborhood. They hadn't talked to neighbors.

JonBenét's *autopsy* was performed on December 27. It showed she'd been strangled and had a skull fracture.

Most Famous Cold Case Ever

For years the Boulder Police Department tried to blame the Ramseys. First they said John did it. Then they said Patsy did it. At one point JonBenét's brother, Burke, was even accused. He was only nine at the time of the murder.

Boulder police didn't have much murder investigation experience. They were also having "turf wars." The FBI had been called in. At first everyone thought the case was a kidnapping. That crime is the FBI's *jurisdiction*. But then they found the body. The case became a murder. The Boulder Police Department took over.

Many people thought an unknown intruder was responsible. But Boulder police kept insisting the Ramseys did it.

New DNA Test May Solve Case

As of 2009, nearly 13 years have passed since JonBenét died. Her murder is one of the world's most famous unsolved cases. But, it may not remain unsolved much longer. A new kind of DNA testing may finally help solve the case.

DNA tests were first used in the late 1980s. At that time, scientists needed a sample the size of a quarter. It could be blood or other bodily material. Later, in the 1990s, scientists only needed a dime-sized sample. Then it got even smaller: "If you can see it, you can analyze it."

Today, the sample doesn't need to be visible at all. A *touch DNA test* can find DNA on anything touched by a person. People leave behind skin cells on everything they touch. The touch DNA test works on just about any kind of surface. It can even work on something rough, like cloth.

Ramseys Cleared

In 2008 this new DNA test was used on JonBenét's clothing. The touch DNA test provided a major break in the case. Scientists found the DNA of an unknown male in two places. It was on JonBenét's underwear and long johns. This confirms the "unknown intruder" idea. Investigators ran the DNA through the FBI's DNA database. So far they haven't found a match.

On July 9, 2008, the Ramseys were cleared. The Boulder County District Attorney officially apologized to John Ramsey. Sadly, Patsy Ramsey died of cancer in 2006. She didn't live to see the family name cleared. She and JonBenét are buried next to each other in Marietta, Georgia.

On February 2, 2009, police officially reopened the case. The FBI continues to recheck the DNA. They hope the killer's DNA will show up in another case. Then they can solve JonBenét's murder.

CHAPTER 3

NATALEE HOLLOWAY

DATAFILE

T I M E L I N E

May 30, 2005

Natalee Holloway disappears on a trip to Aruba.

December 18, 2007

Aruban investigators announce the case is closed.

February 1, 2008

Police reopen the case when a suspect says Holloway is dead.

Where is Oranjestad, Aruba?

K E Y   T E R M S

chaperone—an adult who attends an event to keep young people out of trouble

convulsing—shaking uncontrollably

detain—to hold in police custody

infrared sensor—an electronic device that detects invisible waves

white slavery—forced prostitution

DID YOU KNOW?

Carlos 'n Charlie's is the bar and restaurant where Natalee was last seen. It's part of a chain. Because she disappeared there, the place has been changed to a Señor Frog's. The same company owns both chains.

NATALEE HOLLOWAY

Aruba is a spring-break vacation hotspot. With its exciting nightlife, it's very popular with students. Some think of it as the Caribbean Las Vegas.

This warm, sunny island lies just north of Venezuela. It is part of the Netherlands. Dutch is one of the official languages there. Papiamento is the other. That language comes from Spanish and Portuguese.

In May 2005, a beautiful, blonde American girl went missing there. Her story was splashed all over newspapers.

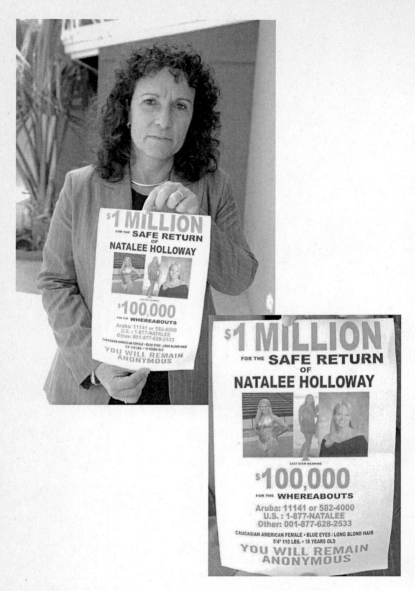

A reward was announced for Natalee Holloway's safe return by the lawyer representing her family.

Everyone wanted to know what happened to her. So far she hasn't been found.

A High School Graduation Trip

Natalee Holloway was a straight-A student. She had been a member of National Honor Society. She was also on the dance team and did other school activities. She was planning to go to the University of Alabama in the fall. She had a full scholarship and was going to study pre-med.

The pretty 18-year-old had just graduated from Mountain Brook High School. It's in a wealthy suburb of Birmingham, Alabama.

Her senior class had planned a graduation trip to Aruba. Natalee and 124 of her fellow graduates arrived in Aruba on May 26, 2005. They were there to party.

The graduates were scheduled to be there for five days. They were staying at a Holiday Inn in Oranjestad, the Aruban capital.

There's safety in numbers, Natalee's parents thought. Other students from her school had gone to Aruba in the past. There had never been any problems. Seven adult *chaperones* went on the trip, too. They were there to make sure the kids were OK.

On the last day, Natalee didn't show up for her return flight. Police found her packed bags and passport in her hotel room. But Natalee was nowhere to be found.

Massive Hunt Begins

Beth Twitty went to Aruba as soon as she learned Natalee was missing. Beth was Natalee's mom. Natalee's parents were divorced, and Beth had remarried. Jug Twitty was her husband. He was Natalee's stepdad. Natalee's dad, David Holloway, also went to Aruba.

Tourism is a major industry in Aruba. The authorities wanted to make sure the island seemed safe. So they began a massive hunt for Natalee.

Posters went up all over. The government gave thousands of employees the day off. That way they could help with the search. Hundreds more volunteers helped, too. Some even came from the United States.

Dutch Marines combed the shoreline. Divers checked the ocean around the island. The Royal Netherlands Air Force even sent three F-16 fighter planes. They were equipped with special *infrared sensors*. The planes were looking for shifts in the ground. These could mean a shallow grave.

Three Suspects

The night before she was to leave Aruba, Natalee had stayed out late. She was hanging out at a popular spot called Carlos 'n Charlie's. She had been drinking.

Natalee's classmates saw her leave with a local 17-year-old boy. Joran van der Sloot was a Dutch honors student. He was at Carlos 'n Charlie's with two Surinamese friends. They were 21-year-old Deepak Kalpoe and his 18-year-old brother Satish. They left with Natalee in Deepak's car around 1:30 a.m.

Police interviewed the three young men the next day. Joran said they had taken Natalee to the beach to look at sharks. After that they drove her back to her hotel. Later their story changed several times.

On June 5, police *detained* two men on suspicion of murder and kidnapping. Antonius "Mickey" John and Abraham Jones had worked as security guards at another hotel. The reason for their arrest has never been clear. Statements by Van der Sloot and the Kalpoe brothers may have been a factor. The two guards had been known to cruise hotels looking for women.

Police released the two men without charges on June 13.

More Searching, More Suspects

Aruban authorities stepped up the search over the next year. Police arrested Van der Sloot and the Kalpoe brothers again. They eventually released the Kalpoes. They held Van der Sloot for several months. He changed his story several times. Finally police decided they didn't have enough evidence. They let him go.

Police investigated a number of other suspects as well. In all, they detained and questioned at least 10 suspects. The FBI was also involved, as were other U.S. law enforcement agencies.

At one point a piece of duct tape was found. It had blonde hairs stuck to it. Detectives thought they might be Natalee Holloway's. They did a DNA test. The hairs were not Natalee's.

Case Closed, Then Reopened

On December 18, 2007, the case was officially closed. The prosecutor said there was not enough evidence. It's difficult to prove anything without a body. Natalee's remains have never been found.

Then, in January 2008, the case was reopened. Dutch crime reporter Peter R. de Vries announced he had solved the case. He said Joran van der Sloot had told him something very interesting.

According to de Vries, the young man had said he was with Natalee when she began *convulsing*. She appeared to be having some kind of reaction to alcohol or drugs. Van der Sloot tried, unsuccessfully, to revive her. He believed she was dead. He then called a friend, who told him to go home. The friend said he would dispose of the body in the ocean.

Van der Sloot's friend denied this ever happened. Then Van der Sloot denied it himself. He said he had been under the influence of marijuana when he said it, and that it was untrue. Van der Sloot at one point also said he had sold Natalee into *white slavery*.

This young man has told many stories. It's hard to tell whether there's any truth to any of them. Today he insists that he left Natalee on the beach, alive. He says he initially lied because he felt ashamed about leaving a young woman alone on the beach. That's what she wanted, though, he said.

As of 2009, Natalee Holloway has not been found. Nor have her remains.

CHAPTER 4

THE ALLEN-CUTSHALL MURDERS

DATAFILE

T I M E L I N E

2002

Lindsay Cutshall and Jason Allen meet in West Virginia.

August 18, 2004

Their bodies are found on a northern California beach.

May 2006

Police release new evidence, hoping for leads.

Where is Mount Hope, West Virginia?

KEY TERMS

evangelical—belonging to a Christian group that believes the Bible is the true word of God

frugal—good at holding onto money and not wasting it

missionary—a person sent by a church to help people and teach them religion

satanic—having to do with Satan or the devil

zodiac—a round diagram showing the 12 astrological signs

DID YOU KNOW?

Alcatraz is a small island in San Francisco Bay. It is home to a famous former prison. These days it is a popular San Francisco tourist attraction. Every day, ferries take tourists to Alcatraz to tour the prison.

THE ALLEN-CUTSHALL MURDERS

Lindsay Cutshall and Jason Allen worked at an outdoor adventure camp called Rock-N-Water. It's an hour east of Sacramento, California.

The camp is for Christian youth. They take part in whitewater rafting. They also do rock climbing, kayaking, and other outdoor sports. And they strengthen their relationship with God.

Lindsay and Jason were very passionate about their work. Lindsay, 22, and Jason, 26, both loved kids. Lindsay would often talk to the camp's young girls until after midnight. She'd help them with their problems and offer support.

The two were planning to marry on September 11, 2004. It was only a few weeks away. They were excited about their upcoming wedding.

Both believed in being *frugal*. Their needs were simple. They even set up their wedding registry at Target. A registry is a list of items a couple needs when they get married. It helps family and friends pick out wedding gifts.

Missionary Work

Jason met Lindsay in West Virginia in 2002. She was a student at Appalachian Bible College in Mount Hope. He was working as a rafting guide nearby. Both were from the Midwest.

Jason had thought he'd never find the perfect woman. He wanted someone who shared his love of nature and God. Lindsay was the woman of his dreams. The daughter of an Ohio *evangelical* minister, she shared Jason's *missionary* values. They both wanted to spread God's word.

Their summer spent working at Rock-N-Water was not just a job. To prepare, Jason had saved up $2,000 for their rafting-guide training. They wanted to own their own adventure camp one day. Both loved whitewater rafting.

A Weekend Getaway

Summer's end was near. Soon the couple would return home for their wedding. They decided to take a weekend trip. Lindsay especially wanted to see San Francisco.

She and Jason packed up their red Ford Tempo. They took camping gear and food. They also brought a camera. They wanted lots of pictures from their trip.

The young couple left Rock-N-Water on Friday night, August 13. They told coworkers they were going to see friends.

They spent most of the next day in San Francisco. Lindsay used her credit card around 1 p.m. She bought a set of tiny Tabasco sauce bottles at Pier 47. Pictures from their camera showed the happy couple visiting San Francisco landmarks. They posed in front of Golden Gate Bridge and toured Alcatraz.

Camping on the Beach

Later that day, Jason and Lindsay headed north. They were traveling the winding roads of Sonoma County. They bought gas in Guerneville. After that, their story gets a little murky. People say they saw them at various locations. But police aren't sure if it was really them.

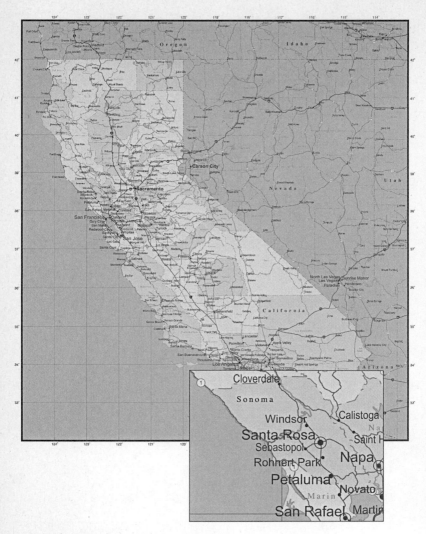

Fish Head Beach is in Sonoma County.

At some point they decided to camp. They found a cozy spot at Fish Head Beach near the tiny town of Jenner. It was cool and misty. There were several huts on the beach. They were made of driftwood that had washed up on shore.

Lindsay and Jason spread out their sleeping bags. A photo of the sunset was the final shot in their camera. The couple spent their last night together on that lonely beach.

But it turned out they were not alone.

Someone murdered them during the night. Jason and Lindsey were shot in the head at close range. There was no indication of a struggle. They were probably shot while they slept. Their belongings were left alone. No one had tried to take their money, jewelry, or camera.

Reported Missing

The couple was due back on Sunday, August 15, at 5 p.m. Their failure to show up was cause for alarm. By the following afternoon, their parents were on their way to California. A missing persons report had been filed.

The couple's bodies weren't found until Wednesday. A helicopter was flying over the area. It was rescuing a teenager from a nearby cliff. The pilot spotted two sleeping bags on the beach. The people in them didn't wake up from the chopper noise. So the pilot landed the helicopter nearby. He checked and found that both people were dead.

Ballistics reports showed the murder weapon was a .45 caliber Marlin rifle. It is a somewhat unusual gun, but not terribly uncommon. Sonoma detectives examined the Marlin rifles of people in the area. None was a match.

Similar Cases

The Sonoma County Sheriff's Department was baffled. There didn't seem to be any motive. These were two fine young people with no known enemies.

There had been similar cases in the past. There was one in Arizona, one in Oregon, and one in Vancouver, British Columbia. But they don't appear to be related. Some people also think it could have been the *Zodiac* Killer. There were similarities, and the Zodiac has never been caught.

New Clues Released

By 2006, the Allen-Cutshall murder case was starting to get cold. It had been two years, and there were no suspects. The police decided to release a few clues to the public. They hoped this would jar people's memories.

One clue was a 40-oz. bottle of Camo beer. It was found near the bodies. This unusual beer was only available at a few stores. Police also revealed a journal left in one of the driftwood huts. Several people had written in it. Detectives asked the people who'd written in it to come forward. So far no one has.

Another clue was two *satanic* etchings on driftwood. These devil-related drawings may have been connected to the crime. They were found near the bodies. Lindsay's father believes satanic activity was involved.

America's Most Wanted profiled the Allen-Cutshall murders on March 17, 2007. So far the killer has not been found.

CHAPTER 5
SOLVED AT LAST

DATAFILE

T I M E L I N E

May 1, 2001

Chandra Levy disappears.

May 1, 2002

Evelyn Hernandez disappears.

December 24, 2002

Laci Peterson disappears.

Where is Modesto, California?

K E Y   T E R M S

arraigned—called before a court to answer charges

closure—bringing to an end

intern—a person who works as a trainee to gain experience

skeletal—having to do with a skeleton or bones

syndrome—a group of related events

DID YOU KNOW?

Scott Peterson was having an affair when his wife, Laci, disappeared. He had told the other woman, Amber Frye, that he was a widower. That was three weeks *before* Laci disappeared. Amber later helped police gather evidence against her former lover. She also wrote a book and appeared on talk shows.

SOLVED AT LAST

Sometimes police finally solve cold cases. Then the detectives' efforts pay off. The culprit is finally caught and punished. The victims' families get *closure*, or a feeling that it's finally over.

Modesto, California, had two very high-profile murders in the early 2000s. Both made headlines all over. One was a cold case that went unsolved for eight years. Police solved the other in less than a year.

Chandra, Laci, and Evelyn

Chandra Levy disappeared in 2001 in Washington, D.C. She had been working there as an *intern*. She grew up in Modesto.

Laci Peterson was also from Modesto. She disappeared right before Christmas in 2002. Laci was seven and a half months pregnant.

Evelyn Hernandez's murder was eerily similar to Laci's. She, too, was nearing the end of her pregnancy. Her body was also found in San Francisco Bay.

But her case didn't get much publicity. The reason may be explained by "missing white woman *syndrome*." Her killer has not been found.

An Intern Goes Missing

Chandra Levy disappeared May 1, 2001. She had been working as an intern in Washington, D.C. The unpaid learning position was at the Federal Bureau of Prisons. She wanted to become an FBI agent.

Her internship was nearly over. Chandra was getting ready to return to California. But then she disappeared without a trace.

On May 5, Chandra's parents called D.C. police. They hadn't heard from their daughter for a few days. They were worried.

Chandra had told her aunt a secret. She was having an affair with a married congressman. His name was Gary Condit. Chandra's father told police about the affair.

A Fruitless Search

On May 10, detectives searched Chandra's apartment. She had visited a Web site on the day she disappeared. It was about Rock Creek Park.

A search party looked for Chandra's body. The body was there in the park, but the search party missed it. A year later, a man found Chandra's *skeletal* remains. He was walking his dog when he found the body. It was just outside the search area.

Gary Condit was never officially a suspect. But the affair destroyed his political career.

Finally, in March 2009, police arrested a suspect. Ingmar Guandique was already doing time for attacking two other women in Rock Creek Park. Guandique was *arraigned* May 27, 2009. He was charged with murder and other crimes. He pleaded not guilty. His trial will be in 2010.

A Sad Christmas Tale

At 27, Laci Peterson was pregnant with her first child. She and her husband Scott had been married for five years. Laci had tried to get pregnant for quite a while. She was about to try fertility drugs. She was happy when she got pregnant naturally.

The baby was a boy. Laci and Scott decided to name their son Conner Latham Peterson. But it wasn't to be.

On December 24, 2002, Laci disappeared. Her husband Scott had gone fishing for the day. When he returned, she wasn't there. So he called her mother. Sharon Rocha hadn't heard from Laci, either. A massive search was begun. More than 1,000 volunteers helped.

A Grisly Discovery

Finally, on April 13, 2003, Conner's infant body was found. A couple walking their dog found the baby's remains on the shore. The body was well preserved, probably from the cold water. A day later, part of Laci's body was recovered.

Scott Peterson was transported to San Quentin Prison's Death Row after he was formally sentenced for the murder of his wife, Laci, and their unborn son.

DNA tests confirmed Laci's and Conner's identities.

Laci's husband Scott was charged with murder shortly after the bodies were found. On March 16, 2005, the court sentenced Scott to death by lethal injection.

Today he is on death row at San Quentin. He is awaiting appeal. He says he is innocent.

Missing White Woman Syndrome

Every year, there are many missing persons cases. Only a few are widely covered in the media. Critics say there's a reason. They call it "missing white woman syndrome." They say the media gives more coverage to wealthy, pretty, young white women. Chandra Levy and Laci Peterson both fit that bill.

Murder is tragic no matter who the victim is. But news stories often help solve cases. Some say news coverage is not equal. But it should be.

Evelyn Hernandez was a young Hispanic woman whose case was similar to Laci's. She was nine months pregnant. She and her 5-year-old son disappeared in San Francisco in 2002. Her body was found in San Francisco Bay. The bodies of her baby and her 5-year-old son have never been found.

Evelyn was unmarried. She was an immigrant from El Salvador. Critics say these are the reasons why her case got little coverage.

Good Morning America anchor Chris Cuomo gave his opinion. He said the media was just giving people what they want.

GLOSSARY

accomplice—someone who helps commit a crime

arraigned—called before a court to answer charges

autopsy—a study done on a dead body to find the cause of death

blacklisted—added to a list of people kept from working in their field

chaperone—an adult who attends an event to keep young people out of trouble

closure—bringing to an end

convulsing—shaking uncontrollably

detain—to hold in police custody

evangelical—belonging to a Christian group that believes the Bible is the true word of God

frugal—good at holding onto money and not wasting it

garrote—a corded device with handles, used for strangling

GLOSSARY

inducted—installed in a group via formal ceremony

infrared sensor—an electronic device that detects invisible waves

intern—a person who works as a trainee to gain experience

jurisdiction—authority over an area's law enforcement

ligature—something used for tying someone up, such as rope or cord

missionary—a person sent by a church to help people and teach them religion

satanic—having to do with Satan or the devil

skeletal—having to do with a skeleton or bones

speculation—guesswork

syndrome—a group of related events

touch DNA test—a new DNA test that can take a DNA sample from an item that was touched

uncooperative—not willing to work together toward a common goal

white slavery—forced prostitution

zodiac—a round diagram showing the 12 astrological signs

INDEX

A

Aerosmith, and Run-DMC, 13–14
Alcatraz (island/prison), 41
Allen, Jason, 6. *See also* Allen-Cutshall murders
Allen-Cutshall murders
  backgrounds of victims, 42, 43–45, 47
  murder, 47
  new clues released (2006), 49–50
  police investigation, 48–49
  reported missing, 48
  timeline of case, 40
Aruba, and the Natalee Holloway case, 31

C

Cold cases, defined, 5
Cutshall, Lindsay, 6. *See also* Allen-Cutshall murders

F

50 Cent, 16–17

H

Hernandez, Evelyn. *See* Modesto, California, crimes in
  case summary, 60

timeline of case, 51
Hip-Hop
  changes in, 13–14
  pioneers in, 12
Holloway, Natalee, 6
  Aruba and, 31, 32–33
  Carlos 'n Charlie's, Aruba, 30
  case closed then reopened, 38–39
  class trip, 33–34
  disappearance, 29
  investigation of disappearance, 34–38
  manhunt for, 34–35
  student life, 33
  suspects in case, 35–38
  timeline of case, 29

J

Jam-Master Jay (a.k.a., "Jazzy Jase"), 5
  birth and early life, 10
  case timeline, 7
  death of, 7, 10, 14–15
  DJing at Two-Fifths Park, 10
  50 Cent and, 16–17
  Run-DMC album, 7, 12–13

INDEX

suspect in murder of, 7, 15

L

Levy, Chandra, 6. *See also* Modesto, California, crimes in
case summary, 54–56
timeline of case, 51

M

McDaniels, Darryl "DMC," 10
McGriff, Kenneth "Supreme," 16–17
Missing persons and the "missing white woman syndrome," 59–60
Modesto, California, crimes in
Hernandez, Evelyn, 54, 60
high profile murders in, 53
Levy, Chandra, 54–56
Peterson, Laci, 56–59
similarities among victims, 54

P

Peterson, Laci, 6. *See also* Modesto, California, crimes in
summary of case, 56–60
timeline of case, 51
Peterson, Scott, 6

R

Ramsey, JonBenét, 6
case reopened, 28
case timeline, 18
DNA testing and, 26–27
discovery she was gone, 23–24
false confession in case, 19
family life, 20–21
first investigation, 23, 25
law enforcement authority, 25–26
parents cleared, 28
Rincon, Tony, 15
Run-DMC
1990s period, 13–14
2001 tour, 14
Aerosmith and, 13–14
start of, 10
success, 12

S

Shakur, Tupac, 10
Simmons, "DJ Run," 10
Smalls, Biggie, 9

W

Washington, Ronald "Tenad," 7, 15
Witnesses
statements of, 15
uncooperative, 16